A YOUNG RECRUIT

D1521310

A YOUNG RECRUIT

Jean Day

ROOF

The author would like to thank the editors of *Abacus, InFolio,*
and *Writing,* where versions of these poems were first published.

ISBN: 0-937804-30-4
Library of Congress Catalog Card No.: 88-090722

Production by Susan Bee
Typeset by Skeezo
Cover art: *Med Vervis* by Liubov Popova, Robert and Maurine
Rothschild Collection.
Author photo by Laura Hartman

This book was made possible, in part, by grants from the
National Endowment for the Arts and the New York State
Council on the Arts.

ROOF BOOKS
are published by
The Segue Foundation
303 E. 8th St.
New York, New York 10009

Table of Contents

figure   5

NO SPRINGS TRAIL

F E E T

N A T U R E   G I R L

F R O M   H A P P Y   E N D

FIGURE

"The joy of my thoughts ... blocking out all else."

Picture

Morning: giant levis salute

whoever they work for

I return the salute and freeze myself to the sand underfoot
which is what? Composed.

The work, it was going to be named after the Junior,
tooling about a little seaport town with a few clues.

Though set in a dangerous time, a trap-door suddenly opens
and voila! This hulk appears with pan-bread in his hands and
a baby on his back.

Interiority coaches a wry person.

Everyone's out of the house, walking or whatever.

Please leave a message.

NO SPRINGS TRAIL

GROUND

Later.

Sections of sky arouse
languid passing
where sheep may safely graze.

Prosaic trees stand
calculated as animation
pours down plot
after plot.

On the grass
as part of a rescue
the teams, domestic and familial
suddenly start &

Into a composite scene
red weekend things
come walking. If you just want to go somewhere
and think

It must have a gripping effect

on people. Power (not suggestion)
darkens the sky. Geese
flock. We thought
you wouldn't stop

to the noise of alot of decoys.
Oh Shenandoah your great
shape destroys its own
arms. Pen-knife points

To nature, called Ranch-Hotel
after it was civilized.
One born there
charts a hot path

through wet
Without refrain.
It seemed clear she couldn't bite
the nipple *off*

though object song
leads closure to lush
garden camellias falling
with birds not bodily

but just. Across deep
green the glory
and the rag fly
writing up a size,

out a window, geometry
proved in thought, tries.
Then these lines swell
to an almost historical rain

founded on our first metaphysical

UNREST

The window is open. Jiggle the picture. Jar the fruit. A big dog
is on its way.

I have no two things
that take from order
order. Fancy too
is bent

converted. Design
by committee passes
fluster through window
across yard

purpose I always
call things. Fidelity
of enough in the land
of that land, fly

through my window my
gone walking
tall trays all trees
little hard
                hard again

I make a care a thing. Trouble. The poem yearns for its personal guardian.

of hearing. It's something
to do to throw a care
away downhill on which
a cow might stand.

The zodiacal light
guards the straitaway,
flanked by roadhouses
full of grub.

Whereas a certain sheen
tears down to build
another ring-device
liking writing better

reading old man's
beard. Rubber digits
lit by moon attract
gaze and then resist

bonus, lakefront
ridge-road calm.
The newsprint mind
slumps to radiate

Perspective plays with readers' gaze. You have to figure out deep space.

collected heat.
neighbors stay
to hand along the hot
hall. Hill with a house

on it. Back up several
paces a composer stands
puffed
like a reputation.

Add-on hours
etruscan red about
pillars thought
into place

want a proud look
stumped and gnarly
through two-way glass
confusing the stars

with cover.
That's why they're called sneakers,
neat. Off the ground
into the air in a cone (away)

I'm digging a ditch with a blindfold on, remembering happy times.

To a horse. Dragged
a travois can not
porte-cochère or trellis.
Her side. They look

and drive away,
the way, looking at them,
green pounds.
Power is power to transform

bramble to a sleeping
porch. Order is order
felt buckle-coats remind
the hand that floors

remain gently scaled,
reproduced as number
in imagination. Is a
career name slant

blanket, too slanted reasonably
to be rain. And there her idea is.
A board and a batten
dug into a hill

Models are better in parts, broken down to irreducible, if absurdly truncated, elements.

How Americans can
and they will distinguish
if able the possible
relation to the rugged

Would it? Wooden.
To speak with
a small cowboy standing outside
the restaurant waiting

for the word. I am
a standup and eventually
like Lacy, *place*
the sacks.

In them, continuation.
I thought so. To undo.
Permit pass you, death.
"Family." Apply science

in the imagination of number.
Mud pond scandalously
out. There, after a fact,
a man, by his man.

I'm not afraid of toys.

Or, after what you knew
I was talking about explodes
before a new
relativism, toy standing outside

like a shadow, then forgetting
the original postures
organs in a team leave
a trail over which we pass.

Permit pass you don't
manage
By which stopped time came
about a "spirited away"

cumbrous over the hilly texture
of road where men
came from in the first place.
That road represented

by a flower arrangement
partly open to sky
part favor, part parted
in division. A shadow

On earth, I too belong.

belonging to a big dog
moves over its shrinking
backward through slant
sun occupying

rascality. Would it
always be so; revision
of the person, revision
of things. Beyond

our lifetime every day
some couplets—a dark European
stripe across the sky—
capable fate

accrues grasp
of the case to bend it
blinded gate closed
beyond likelihood, garden

lying still like two
dimensions. Positive space
enacted through trees plays
handsomely approximate...

B O A T

for RGD

Blood's in the body
Funny   I let *that* go on ...
Phone rings off the book ...
Bulk I'm about
To become   Carolina Wrong, knocks.
Who needs dry socks?

Thinking inside the head
Birdsong: points in a shape
I would like to go boating
Think, who will get
The limited number of kidneys?
My ears cloud over

One by one.
Is it a wall or what will happen?
The success, a scene which is less
In a stall
Loves *things*
Plenty to ride up on, score

Like moon light "always" sciences
Minimum planets in a field of play
Curable eye, imaginable you, thinkable
They rest. Unconcluded by a day's walk—
I hear this bell coming across
Heidi's cookie   Fortunately the sky

Comes short   Blazes wild
Artichoke coming round
The soul as something we can call
Our foot, if it weren't for all that water
Talk about birds! That crashing
Just deer   Howdy, scared of cows

You'd make somebody a nice
Twelve buns
The sun tries to go out, refinishing
Understanding, itself
A nuisance (decreasing
With distance) producing

Tall shorts   That went by like a song
"There is no answer imagining desire"
No dogs   Please close gate
Big kids riding bikes
Big kids, riding bikes
That's a very nice water fountain

Bare always to friendly motion within
Unsung, uneasy, easy, chair   Proud
Of what she'd done   Don't listen
If you haven't heard a rolling rock
Walk, and in one body
Conversed beside a squall

Eventually boys and girls; it's that simple.
This made me remember a part of my mind
Pound piling up my desk, hopeful ducks
In a batch of sunlight
It has snowed deep enough on Oui-Mei
Then I

... I was really on a paint, eat, sleep schedule. It probably paid for some of your education. Material availability happens to matter. My interest is emotional; maybe you are that way too. Plus, the willingness to do alot of grinding, fairing at the welds if there is intelligence and training ... Blasted and primed she will have a five-foot draft, organized with sheers, brakes, nibblers (big ones!); she will be an inboard rig. The last two jobs I am doing for others ... The design I am working on will have four strakes (three strakes), and with this introduction, trees are not the culmination of plant evolution, elevated as they are! ... Shade, you fall across nature.

We drove up the mountain to a nice sit-down there and broke into song. The husband was lumbering carefully along with the drinks in a box. His brothers were asleep wearing short socks and mesh caps. Sham anthropology put them at ease while the women did their dance. That was the meaning of Bluegrass after all, where clouds part and the wind is high and mighty.

It was in a journal written by a monster and read by a clam we learned such precepts as "Trust each others' Trust," or something like that. Obviously what could not be said would never be famous, but we clouds came over to shade our only son, who was at that time a peach. He had said "It's not possible to get where you are overland in two days." And it was *so* with his mother, Autumn, but the voracious wind swallowed up his speech and she returned dejected to her limousine.

In every composition is the community. Clouds part in another place to reveal a person full of ideas, a young female recruit. Using yours, she tries to pass on to another world where mayhem rearranges all our songs:

"But if you ride back and I am dead . . .

" . . . and we shall be where suns are not . . .

"Hello stranger.

New figures crowd the sky above her ramshackle pallet. A man on a horse towers ("Just a girl" he says, to calm the horse). Then she and he and the horse stand in single file separated only by numbers, the last three digits of which don't match. High up the stars blink dimly. One of the writers says, "There was nothing lonely about that trip. There never was on that road." Then draws the lead curtain to a close.

Outside, they ask the psychic, "How do you weave bodies? What is in this rejuvelac?"

"This day this hour this spring —

                                        she says

"Drive this thing!

FEET

STORMY

Those fishing
Don't say a word

A bell is tolling.

These are not real things, just technique.

Reason, a suitcase, may appear loaded.

It is catholic. Says, "These things are past:

Slant, Steel, Drone, Breath, Dune, Leaf ... "

Well it might be good to get hard candy
But not with a jar of water

. . .

The code is simple, so that anyone in prison

(far away from a detail)

Everyone's name is Jack
Everyone's name is Jimmy

(Beauty contains an object in idealism)

. . .

Darkly intimated by a blood tie

a rudely hilarious remark

makes the father. Then sulks the son of man

on hanging rock thinking thickly of a ridge.

A cloud in trousers slaps its hands

to the tune: "Hands Heated Laxity"

lets papers gush

through horizontal slots —

We went on through the motions of phrasing

cows sit down

And when we examine your head there are black paintings,

fancy script, your own name and number:

Tournement Alleys

Drench dredge red
the push. I see letters
pass, little more. A
famous inn I paced with-
in the proud name she
bears. I saw them sort
with such a bird as in
a chain a man can glory.

written all over.

"Open thou my lips."

video, italic

Everyone has smelled a summer night, neither

are we exalted and nobody. A moody wind slaps us up

as The Bitch in The Storm arrives

in her car

and I & she get beyond the object
holding my erection
like boys at the captain's table

And cadence never decomposes all our days.

.   .   .

True, she would have to think about that anchor.

A word problem on the road ("no"

or possibly "on"

in large chalk letters) asks

will she see, say

that plug again? Placard, poem, postcard,

speech:

> "When the rain comes out I'll have fins on
> but don't bother me boys because
> I'll be busy fishing"

Man asks how far to next drinking

fountain, leads this white character to a bench.

I am French.

It is pretty to sit down.

. . .

Love dreamed of course

and as you turn rakish in the L shape,

ideal interior, see manifold

choir stuck on one note,

the boat

then the river

Lookouts,
they walked to the stars with rings on
from one ravaged decade to the next

direct-hit by

looking through some peephole
on Oral Roberts' transparent socks

. . .

Someone shoves a hand-crafted brochure to Nature

(Nature Girl), in my face. The weather warm

always already in retrospect.

I had been in the mossy dent but preferred a nearby body

of water. Critiqued by the great romantic-modernist

critic we become glamour-rustic and usually rub

each other awhile. I stop at all the chairs.

Some dangerous people (Johnny Torch, Sue Storm,

and "Fireball") follow, but suppose they too

only wish to gallop

without one quiet thought?

. . .

ONE SHADE FRAGMENTS FORTY
AT   GREAT   MEAT   SALE

.   .   .

A short Living-Legend moves fast across a place

to give a general view of the interior.

> I wore my dress.
>
> I was somebody out for a walk
> amorously wrecking down hot
> where she wants to sit in your shadow.
> There was no one else in the watershed
> but ragged, late-season swifts,
> swallows. His was bright advice
> to use Groucho Marx's style
> going downhill. Then refill.
> Boy Scouts had been there, pine cones
> and all. Then I fell down.
>
> *"Well, hello, baby."*

Large wood (wooden) abuts

> Not that abyss
>
> *alot of fun there.*

Howling, the baby flies into the water (whose community was *that*)?

> This same fountain
> your American town
> gave the past a life
> see where it takes the vertical

future. And the girls hold up the trees (their fathers) I think,

in the ancient way, smiling, . . . still smiling . . .

> Solid.

. . .

"The body, not an object but a condition of passion."

. . .

They used to think intervention made the leaves unfold

Now the urgent voice-over guns ventilator fans.

The speech is never over.

The cut-out in the wings has to comb

his or her hair.

Obligatory mate says "Why so happy honey?"

"I'm thinking about tomorrow."

Girls, consigned

to amusing re-runs, lash together to form a raft:

> Buzz adjust end-to-end
> side by side dawn's birds
> bulky from the tomb
> act fickle.
> Her dew
> is on the flower, weltering.
> Mighty is the charm
> of pure intelligence.

. . .

When the Living-Legend's watch beeps he says, "What's that noise?"

. . .

She says, "I'm going over to the house to plug the owl in"

before her final drive.

> What's beyond deep is dark
> Beyond that ruins

Next-door, tightly restrained groups of girls are drawing,

being seen drawing,

many thousands in the yard that day.

One Nation.

.   .   .

"No hiking, horseback riding, dogs."

.   .   .

I suggest a short walk down to the river where blues is king

but get embarrassed when it becomes obvious

it's just my hat

talking to my boot.

> Place, place name, built up,
> peopled world.
> Condensed in ten inches
> of t-shirt.
> "Coca is shit," says Xenia
> The Real Thing, the message,
> Go steal
> and rob, steal and rob . . .

Don't even consider The Sublime!

(legs, lugged uphill)

Then, in the *machine:*

A slender Grecian maiden
tries to think
between two Norse giants.
A carefree theme gathers
a hefty sound

(DON'T I WANT TO BE SAVED???)

Sandwiches in "the going across"
with "the flopping sideways
as it comes to rest."

It was that fifties moderne item he wanted me to wrest

from nature when he sang

"Grab the sword!"

. . .

Don't worry about going back, just wave.

I'm with my group.

Talking on the phone this way any summer night.

Cleaning up the garden-room with water

running down a slope. Slope itself.

Joking. That telephone is ringing in your head

or portion — arousing regard

you counteract   so that:

a queue of timid wrecks *gallops*

beside (do we even *have* that book?)

Admit, resist, receive, overcast.

Great gusts detach seed-pods from their stems.

                    wrong again,
                    which is part of their attraction.

NATURE GIRL

RIVER STICKS

First I fashion a model:
                    O bury my head
while a discrete version stands
                    confident as at a depot
thanks to you and to your friends

The mainstream
                    slips, stumbles, falls
A shuffle between two people that's
                    all I get
out of strange silent dancing

From underground the reflexives
                    and their ants pour; light
realizes day. Birds here bone
                    on variation. A scrambled gloss
may address you. Get in

The singer hesitates and goes back
                    to zero, such as it exactly
was. We take up the barbie and turn it
                    180 degrees. The slope is
covered with description.

Sticking tight to a particular story
                    lyric spins off to someone
"very happy." This person knows how much to fix the bike
                    then engine
—the rest is scrambled glass

Shrinking place to flowered border
          a wine five years
in the can, once called romantic crisis, now called
          strum and drag makes the glass
tremble, the glass on the table

Shake. No more reading. The constellation's
          triangles. Pillbox hut
after thought. I'm not a wolf
          but still I live in a cave
beside *itself*

Talk about sticks
          ladders. O bury my hat
at moist. Film San Francisco
          The drip on the side of the cup's
the lips' leaving

Menace of song
          cup undrunk, beauty
crashed. Name makes the music
          of oblivion. The raft is
lashed and sutured here and there

And nowhere heels to congregation
          sailing on alone along
the surface. A man who looks like a man
          named Mac on Knott's Landing
on TV (also alone on the trail)

Smiles at me. That's where you want to go
                to be with some little pygmies—
seven eights or eight sevens or the many irons
                put to everyone
familiar on the trail. I feel you just need

To push off against. Find the tiny place
                made on you
with my head. Consigned as it is to extravagant
                strangeness, my first name
is knowledge! There's where you want to go to be

Stabled, lean, in each other's neighborhood.
                A luxurious exit should be near
the union of opposites. There are no politics
                in the mind where the other
life does not impinge. She saw the domain

Of song, tuned in his head from the back
                of her mind. The buzz
hurts the saw. A dialectic doesn't operate
                on two red dogs. Still
you would make a nice somebody.

                Clouds went down where the water drinks
                        like cherry wine. Much
                is at first promised, that person's
                        makeral lips fronting
                express intention on a plate. Take them

Opposite. A foreign uniform slides to rest
          sits to the slower thing
the country brings. I! In its aegis!
          Un-reinforced along the way
comes to an abrupt halt. The mouth fantasizes

Rejoinder in an oath. Hours out of sequence
          her teeth her
army story. Fury: by whom she
          has gods.
They need towels and jackets.

When we are all very happy and addicted to tea
          not abstract parties
let's play some trash and some particular.
          Let's go over the famous names before
we find out different about the last

Times the very last, a bend
          around murk. I help you
looking hard at partners in tabloid
          while someone else just comes
around back and punches you

Into two small pictures. That way performance attacks.
          Wait for some more wind
to rattle in, smirking down the street, leaving the world
          in the thrift store. Huge staged war
fits the fist back into the sea's

Grim, red, determined, set on your course
                    canoe. Marked "reckless counsel."
I saw a bright house from the ditch (where two
                    were writing together). Chance
unites her sexual foot with the constant freeway

Anywhere you might choose to cloud your ears.
                    It seems revision is something
to pass the summer in a torpor sitting split
                    at pleasure
on the porch, set on your plate of grass

(Suggesting fresh honey-banded fish
                    in cans and their own wish
to return to hills
                    I thought I could read
all the way across.

          A silent nod from the passerby
                    gives me the go-ahead
          to set off into the mounted diploma.
                    I play
          doll-guitar to use up

          An act. The slightly desirous bees
                    turn on the flower
          in a dark time lasting longer than a single night
                    making her green
          money. Another bug puts the screws on trees

Built to last. Talk about shirts, sweaters.
What means
go by this? Free my hedge from my hat
last civilian
Idea, lead on

"From Momentary Work, A Wrench … "

From momentary work, a wrench, to just fall forward,
conversational birds as cover, answer.

We don't have to speak to the sky, nor streets en route
to roads. Taught to think in rockets'

red, improved individuals double with goods.

She is already good, in one frame a dish,

another a storm. The fly-wheel keeps them coming;

a place to meet a dive

"Bird," "Kingfish." Two who meet re-organize.

Others do significant work, sign, in dubious relation
in weather, to words, under pressure, pushed apart.
And certainly changed. A carving mellows the wood
while one of us tells about the Big Man, the Poet, entering

the operating theater, barechested. That was his job. At least
it was a place to go, a thing to do

after basketball. But they, the Bigger Boys, had broken our
horse by overplaying, and in its place lay a shark,

keys inside, motor running.

Storms warn science fiction mind in motion,
that these original essays culled or spoken from a book
embellish its applied use. The chair on the rug
faces opposite a wall. It is a success. The phone
ringing is the caller's *please.* It's for you
the world is pieces. Feast your eyes on trees
blowing like all get out next to some dead farm
implement. The pilot lights. Please call that number
in my repertoire. Then will you have done?

Deposed by discouraged workers, I, a mother's lament
am a salon favorite. The prodigious lead the way back
to the mere, increments, not a method of work
but reproduction. Door slams as cyclist rides off
under helmet. "You! You!" the savages call
dressed casually to impart confidence in the viewer.
I would be happy to sit in vertical stripes near the buzzer
or just keep track of the proposals (No. 99,999 ...).
A tiny triangle (the instrument) hides in a bean.

Yet again do I seek this quiet spot. Where opposite
a man, a woman, and an automobile. Rain not
raining, a clearing. Start over, stack, reduced
to notes. Make me strong, Story. The rest of life
plays ball in tiny relief. There is no
guarantee or stick of furniture, though to suffer
(but that part is smooth?) out into another
world of preference and work, is a city. As frontier
triggers happy chaos, I am my own vogue.

And so a fog reigns, problems, focus. A step out engages

simple gears, back later, after work, relief

in our renewability, just move that ear a few inches

over here. I have every reason to bite, you, eventually,

to fly. The wraparound itself a relief, chute, papoose.

That's much better than a glass of milk. You going to sing that?

You going to sing that after song? Don't forget

to take a few little things with you, stick

for sudden lameness, oil, should every working part freeze.

We have to have the kinds of things we need.

We should understand it will cost money. We want a flame

to burst out laughing

but it is too expensive. We exert

until a bone leaves (exact the falsetto is not).

I've made a clear spot. Now you. Junk attracts

its veil of crumpled letters. Pure thought falls flat; we fall

injuring others. Miss the point.

In that country they have automobiles too.

FROM HAPPY END

THE RADICAL IS SUBLIME

for Alex Smith

Tell us what to do: act mean, be crazy, stay one step ahead of the critique.

They will try to make us feel bronze: ancient, anaesthetized, and useless but we have things on our mind like Orion's legs.

You are not excused.

Unstable is another term they will use.

It has the same purpose.

Will the transcendent moment never end?

Scene:

WHAT ARE WE GOING TO DO TO YOU NOW? (Voices behind a fiberglass curtain).

"Use strong language!"

Return to your own form.

It will look like you've been asleep the whole time and no one will know the difference.

The public can be divided into two groups. Then two more groups.

Thus, draining the lake.

NIGHT WEARS ON BEHIND THE COLUMNS.

Scene:

NOTHING IS REALLY HAPPENING IN THE WARM ROOM.

A few secretaries (their union: W.O.W.) tap pencils seriously, waiting for the sprocket to lurch one frame forward. Thinking about corn in a groove or one of the other plates from the book. Places you might slip if your shoe doesn't fit. *No one* must see the boss.

Leather-drag hides the irresistible discomfort of the body.

A customer's boots on the plump statue heighten his gorgeous empty eyes.

WHEN A METAPHOR FINALLY APPEARS I WRITE "NICE" IN THE MARGIN

The daily is abstract

to anybody else.

Scene:

Her strapless gown a politically-correct line leads to the rowdy man who grabs a plaster Venus in the Italian restaurant covering it with kisses. He is frenzy. And so I feel let down.

Yet they couldn't figure out how her entire image, roses, rays and all, could jump directly from the man's apron to the great painting now in the cathedral fingered by everybody.

Possibly the ears are not worn *over* the hair?

The present isn't organized in its own mansion, as minks making love obviously are in theirs.

> A man is on – a hotel room
> She wants to be a lamp – reach across
> Huge windows – whose drives
> Finish night thoughts.

Scene:

When she came down from Montana

on that donkey, a woman with a history,

a terrific gale was in progress. She said

she wanted a whole room (with food and drink in it)

to rest in from her labor

in the land of wind and water

where they earn wings every day.

"Citizens! Ours will be the most beautiful of cities!"

<table>
<tr><td>Who's that at
back door sun
fading?</td><td>Who's that at
back door fading
son?</td></tr>
</table>

What are they saying up there?

Scene:

THE ORIGINAL, EVENING, BIRDS

DISTRIBUTION

The mind, excited by television, watches its new problems.

> *reading, sorting, writing, done*
> *reading, sorting, writing, done*

I understood. The paternal last-name system

melted away and as we began to climb

I tired of this company.

Shaking running hair all wild

it was swim or die

or gridlock.

> and I melt her gloves
> and I melt her shoes
> and the snow goes up in the sky

A dog sits under its chair.

The city looked peaceful and true from the airport.

He was awkwardly leaning against a wall, dormant

when I showed up.

The bedroom had been wheeled out into the sun for our pleasure

and for our benefit.

to catch the wave   you apply

        broken off at both beginning and end

Driver and his boy get out, machete in one hand, flashlight

                        in the other.

At the border

    Guard says:

"What you going to do with those Halloween masks?"

              Wear pajamas?   *In the Memory Theater?*

And there *is* no better reason for preferring this elderberry

                        bush.

Unwilling to trade mobility for sexuality, the choice was made

                        in form.

Unevaluated.

Film-people sit at a bar. It's their dog, and he's allowed

                        to sit there too.

But I had meant to precede all this:

> Vacation.
> Lesson.
> Moving fun
> in the old world.

You may not abstract the life of the worker.

She wakes up with the weight of the world

> > on her left arm

which has been having its own dream

> *happy in the face of dread.*

> Dear Bottom,

> > Early morning rapido between Vienna & Munich.
> > Direct, helpful and assured city transport conveys with
> > the stress of a sigh from door to door.
> > We hope you will come, somehow, to see us, when
> > the new complex is built. *We'll be convenient.*

> > I believe in water

> > *management*

> > and that is relevant

> > but really I think I'm jealous

of what I can't *have*

in my own head.

A deep tonic sleep re-arranges our direction.

We are flying over Metropolis again

pointing out which towers have strayed

from a birch or young maple forest.

The compass helps us compose.

A warbler sings two notes up, one down; how do we know these

are just platitudes?

Though instrumental to the work of memory

they support the foregone news of the commander's

watch,

Elegy's battle.

Let the beat, (call it singing)

beat.

Then realize the door to that part of the brain is now closed.

Quiet down.

I *showed* the clouds how to cover up that big blue sky

with the meager tools at my disposal

Then I changed into my other uniform

for the great naming ceremony   which is

an elaborate borrowing act

of community   selecting these

my next thoughts